Randy Moss

by Arlene Bourgeois Molzahn

Reading Consultant:
Dr. Robert Miller
Professor of Special Education
Minnesota State University, Mankato

CAPSTONE
HIGH-INTEREST
BOOKS

an imprint of Capstone Press
Mankato, Minnesota

Capstone High-Interest Books are published by Capstone Press
151 Good Counsel Drive, P.O. Box 669, Mankato, Minnesota 56002
http://www.capstone-press.com

Library of Congress Cataloging-in-Publication Data
Molzahn, Arlene Bourgeois.
   Randy Moss/by Arlene Bourgeois Molzahn.
   p. cm.—(Sports heroes)
   Includes bibliographical references (p. 45) and index.
   Summary: Traces the life and football career of All-Pro wide receiver
Randy Moss.
   ISBN 0-7368-1053-6
   1. Moss, Randy—Juvenile literature. 2. Football players—United States—
Biography—Juvenile literature. [1. Moss, Randy. 2. Football players. 3. African
Americans—Biography.] I. Title. II. Sports heroes (Mankato, Minn.)
GV939.M67 M65 2002
796.332'092—dc21   2001003635

Editorial Credits
Matt Doeden, editor; Timothy Halldin, cover and interior designer ; Katy Kudela,
   photo researcher

Photo Credits
ALLSPORT PHOTOGRAPHY/Vincent Laforet, 4; Brian Bahr, 7; Scott Halleran, 9;
   Harry How, 12; David Gonzalez, 21, 22; Rick Stewart, 25; Elsa Hasch, 30;
   Jonathan Daniel, 32; M. David Leeds, 39
AP/Wide World Photos/Robert Fish, 40
SportsChrome-USA/Steve Woltman, 10, 26; Vincent Manniello, 15, 35; Rob
   Tringali Jr., cover, 17, 42; Mark Friedman, 28; 36
The Sporting News/Phil Coale, 18

1 2 3 4 5 6 07 06 05 04 03 02

Table of Contents

CHAPTER 1

Breakout Victory

On October 5, 1998, a cold rain fell on Green Bay, Wisconsin. Wind blew across Lambeau Field as the Green Bay Packers and Minnesota Vikings took the field. The game was broadcast around North America on *Monday Night Football*. Viking wide receiver Randy Moss was playing in only his fifth NFL game. Many football fans had never seen him play.

Packer fans filled the stadium. The Packers and the Vikings were tied for first place in the NFC Central Division. Both teams had 4-0

Randy scored two touchdowns to help the Vikings beat the Packers 37-24.

records. The Packers also had won 25 games in a row at home. Two more wins would give them the NFL record for consecutive home wins.

Neither team scored a touchdown in the first quarter. The Vikings kicked a field goal late in the quarter to take a 3-0 lead.

In the second quarter, the score was 10-10. Viking quarterback Randall Cunningham threw a high pass to Randy. Randy jumped over his defender and caught the ball. He then ran to the end zone for a 52-yard touchdown.

Later in the second quarter, Cunningham threw to Randy again. Randy reached over his defender and caught the ball. Randy ran downfield toward the end zone. He did not score on the play. But he gained 41 yards and set up another Viking touchdown.

The Vikings held a 30-10 lead early in the fourth quarter. Cunningham found Randy again. He threw a high pass deep into the end zone. Randy's defender jumped for the ball. But Randy grabbed the ball and scored another

Many football experts believe Randy is the best wide receiver in the NFL today.

touchdown. The Vikings led 37-10. The Packers scored two touchdowns late in the game to make the final score 37-24.

Randy caught five passes in the game for 190 yards. The game helped make him one of the most popular players in the NFL.

About Randy Moss

Many football experts believe that Randy is the best wide receiver in the NFL today. He has great speed, excellent jumping ability, and good hands. Few defenders can cover him one-on-one. Randy often makes some of his best catches against double or triple coverage. Randy's skills have made him the most successful young receiver in NFL history. No receiver has ever had more yards or touchdowns in his first three seasons.

In July 2001, Randy signed a new contract with the Vikings. He agreed to play eight more years in Minnesota. The contract will pay him more than $75 million. This figure made Randy the highest paid receiver in NFL history.

CAREER STATISTICS

Randy Moss

NFL Receiving Statistics

Year	Team	Games	Catches	Yards	AVG	Long	TDs
1998	MIN	16	69	1,313	19.0	61	17
1999	MIN	16	80	1,413	17.7	67	11
2000	MIN	16	77	1,437	18.7	78	15
Career		48	226	4,163	18.4	78	43

CHAPTER 2

The Early Years

Randy Moss was born February 13, 1977, in Rand, West Virginia. His mother's name is Maxine. She was a single parent. Randy also has an older half-brother named Eric.

Maxine worked as a nurse's aide. The job did not pay much. Maxine sometimes worked extra hours to earn money for her family. These extra hours meant that she could not spend much time with Randy. She worried about him. Maxine had strict rules for Randy. She made him go to church three times each week. She did not allow him to curse.

Randy was born February 13, 1977.

Jerry Rice

Randy enjoyed watching many athletes when he was young. He watched both basketball players and football players. One of his favorite athletes was wide receiver Jerry Rice.

Rice was a star receiver at Mississippi Valley State University. The San Francisco 49ers selected him in the first round of the 1985 NFL Draft. Rice went on to become one of the greatest receivers in NFL history. He holds almost every league receiving record. After the 2000 season, Rice had 19,247 receiving yards. He had scored 176 receiving touchdowns and 186 total touchdowns. Rice helped the 49ers win three Super Bowls. He was the MVP of Super Bowl XXIII. Rice also played for the Oakland Raiders.

Randy did not have a father at home. He looked up to Eric instead. Eric was a good student and athlete. He played football and basketball.

Randy wanted to be like his brother. He played the same sports that Eric played. Randy discovered that he was an excellent athlete. He could run fast and jump high.

High School

The small town of Rand did not have its own schools. Children from Rand attended school in the nearby town of Belle. In 1991, Randy began his first year at DuPont High School in Belle.

Randy stood out in school. He was already 6 feet (1.8 meters) tall. Most of the students knew that Randy was a great athlete.

Randy soon became a star on DuPont's football team. He played both offense and defense. His favorite position was wide receiver. Randy's speed and jumping ability made him difficult to cover.

Randy also played other sports. He was an excellent basketball player. His height and jumping ability made him a star. Randy also played center field for the baseball team and ran for the track team.

High School Star

Randy quickly became famous throughout West Virginia. Many people thought that he was the best athlete in the state. Randy played on the basketball team with guard Jason Williams. Today, Williams plays in the NBA. Randy was named West Virginia's High School Basketball Player of the Year in both 1994 and 1995.

Randy was even better on the football field. In 12th grade, college football coaches from around the United States came to West Virginia to watch Randy play. The coaches noticed his size, speed, and good hands. Many coaches said he was one of the best high school receivers in the country. Randy was named

People quickly noticed Randy's athletic ability.

West Virginia's 1994 High School Football Player of the Year.

One college coach who recruited Randy was Notre Dame's Lou Holtz. Notre Dame has one of the best college football programs in the United States. Randy agreed to accept a scholarship from Notre Dame. The scholarship would pay for Randy's college expenses while he played football.

You learn from your mistakes, and you've got to pay for them. I've paid for them. Life goes on.
—Randy Moss, AP, 7/27/98

A New Path

In March 1995, one of Randy's friends was involved in a fight at DuPont High School. Randy jumped into the fight to help his friend. But the fight got out of control. Several people were badly hurt. Police officers came to the school to break up the fight. They arrested Randy and several other students. Randy was charged and convicted of battery for taking part in the fight. DuPont High School expelled Randy. He was not allowed to return to school.

Notre Dame officials worried about Randy's behavior. They decided not to give Randy a scholarship. But Holtz still believed that Randy could be a great football player. He talked to Florida State University (FSU) coach Bobby Bowden about Randy. Bowden then offered Randy a scholarship to attend FSU. Bowden told Randy that he could play for FSU if he sat out his first year. Randy agreed. In 1995, he began college classes at FSU.

Randy dreamed of playing wide receiver in the NFL.

CHAPTER 3

The College Years

Randy's days at FSU began well. He attended classes and worked on his studies. In spring 1996, he took part in the football team's spring practice. Bowden and his staff were impressed with Randy's skills. They looked forward to Randy playing an important role on the team during the next year.

Another Change

Randy returned to Rand for the summer. He attended some classes at the College of West Virginia. But Randy made another bad

Randy practiced with FSU's football team during his first year of college.

decision that summer. He smoked some marijuana at a party one night. Two days later, Randy had to take a drug test. The marijuana showed up on the test. Randy again was in trouble for breaking the law. Bowden took away Randy's scholarship at FSU.

Randy had to spend some time in jail that summer. While there, he wrote a letter to Bob Pruett. Pruett had been an assistant coach at FSU. Marshall University in West Virginia had recently hired him to coach the school's football team. Marshall University had a Division I-AA team. Division I-AA is the second highest level of college football.

Pruett told Randy that he could play football at Marshall. Pruett told Randy that he would not accept any bad behavior. Randy promised to stay out of trouble.

A Great Year

Randy joined Marshall for the 1996 season. Marshall's team nickname is the Thundering Herd. In the first game, Randy caught

Randy played wide receiver for the Thundering Herd at Marshall University.

three touchdown passes. He later scored four touchdowns in a game against The Citadel. Randy scored in every game that season. He finished the regular season with 19 touchdowns.

The Thundering Herd advanced to the Division I-AA playoffs. The team's first game

was against the University of Delaware. Randy scored three touchdowns and had 288 receiving yards to lead Marshall to victory. The next game was against Furman University. Randy scored two touchdowns. He scored another touchdown in the next round against the University of Northern Iowa.

Marshall faced the University of Montana in the Division I-AA championship game. Randy caught four touchdown passes for 220 yards. He also ran for a 32-yard touchdown. Marshall won the game 49-29.

Randy scored 28 receiving touchdowns during the 1996 season. That mark tied a Division I-AA record set by Jerry Rice in 1984. Randy also set records with 1,074 receiving yards and a 34-yard average on kickoff returns.

Division I

In 1997, Marshall became a Division I football team. Division I is the top level of college football. The Thundering Herd would face

Randy caught four touchdown passes in the Division I-AA championship against Montana.

more difficult competition as a Division I school. The Thundering Herd joined the Mid-America Conference (MAC).

The competition did not affect Randy's play. He caught 25 touchdown passes during the season. This mark set a MAC record. The previous record had been 13. He ranked third among all receivers in Division I with 2,178 all-purpose yards.

Randy's performance led the Thundering Herd to the MAC championship. The team was invited to play in a bowl game. The Thundering Herd faced the University of Mississippi in the Motor City Bowl. Randy had six catches in the game. One of the catches went for an 80-yard touchdown.

Randy was honored after the 1997 season. He won the Biletnikoff Award as the top receiver in college football. Randy also finished fourth in the Heisman Trophy voting. The Heisman Trophy is the highest individual honor in college football. The award goes to

Randy and the Thundering Herd played against Division I teams in 1997.

the best college player each year. Few players from schools as small as Marshall ever finish that high in the voting.

Randy was pleased with his performance at Marshall. He decided that he was ready to play professional football. Randy announced that he would enter the 1998 NFL Draft.

CHAPTER 4

A Minnesota Viking

Many football experts believed Randy would be one of the top picks in the draft. NFL scouts were excited about his skills. Many believed that he was the best wide receiver to enter the draft in years.

Draft Disappointment

Randy was excited to be drafted. He wanted to be one of the first players chosen. He knew that he had the skills to be a great NFL receiver. But the first five picks passed without Randy being selected.

Randy joined the Minnesota Vikings after they selected him in the 1998 NFL Draft.

Viking receiver Cris Carter helped teach Randy about playing in the NFL.

The Dallas Cowboys had the eighth pick. Dallas had been interested in Randy. Randy was sure that the Cowboys would pick him. But the Cowboys picked defensive end Greg Ellis. Randy was very disappointed.

The 20th pick came. Randy was still waiting. Football experts could not believe that Randy was still waiting to be picked. No one thought Randy's problems off the field would hurt him so much in the draft. The Detroit Lions had the 20th pick. But the Lions selected defensive back Terry Fair.

Finally, the Minnesota Vikings selected Randy with the 21st pick. His wait was over. He was disappointed that so many teams had not picked him. He would have earned more money if he had been picked earlier. But he also was glad to be going to Minnesota to play for coach Dennis Green. The Vikings had a powerful passing offense. Randy vowed to make the teams that passed on him sorry.

Joining the Vikings

Randy joined the Vikings for their training camp before the 1998 season. His brother also joined the team as a guard. Eric was not a star player. He did not play often. But Randy was glad to have him on the team.

Randy quickly became friends with Viking receiver Cris Carter. Carter was one of the Vikings' team leaders. He also was one of the best wide receivers in NFL history. Like Randy, Carter had been in trouble when he was

young. Carter wanted to help Randy get past his troubles. Carter spent a great deal of time talking to Randy and teaching him moves on the football field.

Randy practiced hard. He learned the plays quickly. His teammates were impressed with his skills. The Vikings played a scrimmage game against the New Orleans Saints. Randy scored six touchdowns in this warm-up game. In four pre-season games, Randy caught 14 passes for 223 yards. Green was very pleased with Randy's performance.

A Great Season

Randy's first regular season game was September 6, 1998, against the Tampa Bay Buccaneers. His first NFL touchdown came on a great catch. Viking quarterback Brad Johnson underthrew the ball. Randy had to come back to prevent the defender from making an interception. He tapped the ball. He then ran forward and grabbed it before it landed. Moments later, he ran into the end zone for the

Randy helped the Vikings to a 31-7 win over Tampa Bay in his first NFL game.

The Vikings beat Arizona to advance to the NFC Championship.

touchdown. Randy scored another touchdown later in the game. The Vikings won 31-7.

NFL fans were surprised that Randy had played so well in his first NFL game. Few rookies have the skills to contribute to their teams right away.

Randy and the Vikings had a great regular season. On Thanksgiving Day, they played the

Dallas Cowboys. Randy wanted to prove to the Cowboys that they had made a mistake by not picking him in the draft. He scored three touchdowns in the game. One touchdown was for 51 yards. The other two each were for 56 yards. The Vikings won the game 46-36.

The Vikings finished the season 15-1. They were only the third team ever to finish with such a good record. Randy had 17 touchdown catches that year. No rookie had ever caught that many touchdown passes. He also had 1,313 receiving yards. He was named NFL Rookie of the Year. He also was selected to play in the Pro Bowl.

Disappointment

The Vikings beat the Arizona Cardinals in their first playoff game. They advanced to the NFC Championship to play the Atlanta Falcons. Most experts believed that the Vikings would win the game and advance to the Super Bowl.

The Vikings began the game very well. Randy scored an early touchdown on a 31-yard pass. The Vikings led 20-7. But a fumble near the end of the first half allowed the Falcons to score an easy touchdown. The Falcons were down by only six points at halftime.

The Vikings held a seven-point lead late in the fourth quarter. Viking kicker Gary Anderson had a chance at a 38-yard field goal. Anderson had not missed a kick all year. A field goal would give the Vikings a safe lead. But Anderson missed the kick. The Falcons then drove the field and tied the game. In overtime, the Falcons kicked a field goal to win the game 30-27. The Vikings' season was over.

The 1999 Season

Many football experts believed the Vikings would be the NFL's best team in 1999. But the season was a disappointment for the team. The Vikings had a 10-6 record during the regular season. They beat the Dallas Cowboys in their first playoff game. But they lost to the St. Louis Rams in the second round of the playoffs.

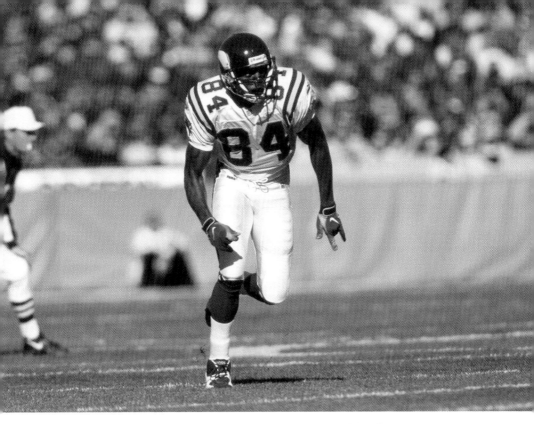

Randy caught 11 touchdown passes and had 1,413 receiving yards in 1999.

Randy had a great individual season. He had seven 100-yard games. He had 1,413 receiving yards and caught 11 touchdowns. He even threw a touchdown pass against the New York Giants on December 26. He again was selected to play in the Pro Bowl. There, he caught nine passes for 212 yards. He was named the game's MVP.

CHAPTER 5

Randy Moss Today

Randy is one of the best receivers in the NFL today. Most experts agree that no other receiver has Randy's combination of size, speed, and athletic ability.

Ups and Downs

Randy and the Vikings had another good season in 2000. The Vikings had a new starting quarterback named Daunte Culpepper. Randy and Culpepper quickly became one of the best quarterback-receiver combinations in

---

Many football experts believe Randy is the best receiver in the NFL.

the NFL. They led the Vikings to an 11-6 record and an NFC Central Division title.

In 2000, Randy caught 77 passes for 1,437 yards. He also scored 15 touchdowns. The Vikings again advanced to the playoffs.

The Vikings' first playoff game was against the New Orleans Saints. Randy caught two passes for 121 yards and two touchdowns.

The Vikings' next game was the NFC Championship in New York against the Giants. Most experts believed that the Vikings would win the game and advance to the Super Bowl. But the Giants scored on their first possession. The Vikings then fumbled the following kickoff. The Giants got the ball back and scored again. The Vikings trailed 14-0 before the offense even took the field. The day did not get better for Randy or the Vikings. They lost 41-0. Randy had two catches for only 18 yards.

Randy and the Vikings suffered another loss in training camp before the 2001 season. On July 31, the Vikings held practice on a hot day. Offensive lineman Korey Stringer became sick

Randy was disappointed after the Giants beat the Vikings 41-0 in the NFC Championship.

I still represent (West Virginia) with everything that I have, and hopefully, one day I'll come back and do something bigger for the state.
—Randy Moss, AP, 7/3/99

from the heat. An ambulance took him to the hospital. Stringer died of heat stroke early the next day. Stringer was one of Randy's best friends on the team.

Off the Field

Randy still enjoys playing basketball. In May 2001, he played basketball for the Pennsylvania Valley Dawgs of the U.S. Basketball League (USBL). Randy scored seven points in his first game. But he later decided to quit the league and concentrate on football.

Randy spends some of his free time with children in Minnesota and West Virginia. He visits sick children in hospitals. He started a program at St. Joseph's Home for Children in Minneapolis, Minnesota. The program is called Randy's Purple Pioneers. Randy speaks to children at St. Joseph's about dealing with problems and having self-confidence. Randy also speaks to children in West Virginia. He tries to show children that they can succeed in life if they work hard.

In May 2001, Randy scored seven points in a USBL basketball game.

Career Highlights

1977—Randy is born February 13 in Rand, West Virginia.

1991—Randy begins playing football at DuPont High School.

1994—Randy is named West Virginia High School Football Player of the Year; he also is named West Virginia High School Basketball Player of the Year.

1995—Randy begins college at Florida State University.

1996—Randy joins the Thundering Herd at Marshall University; he catches 28 touchdown passes and leads Marshall to the Division I-AA championship.

1997—Randy sets the MAC record with 25 touchdowns; he wins the Biletnikoff Award as the top receiver in the NCAA; he finishes fourth in the Heisman Trophy voting.

1998—Randy is drafted in the first round by the Minnesota Vikings; he sets a rookie record with 17 receiving touchdowns; he is named NFL Rookie of the Year.

1999—Randy throws a touchdown pass in a game against the New York Giants.

2000—In January, Randy is named the Pro Bowl MVP.

2001—Randy signs an eight-year contract with the Vikings for more than $75 million.

Words to Know

battery (BAT-uh-ree)—a crime in which one person attacks another

contract (KON-trakt)—a legal agreement between a team and a player; contracts determine players' salaries.

expel (ek-SPEL)—to force a student to leave school

recruit (ri-KROOT)—to try to convince someone to join a team; college football coaches recruit high school players to play on their teams.

rookie (RUK-ee)—a first-year player

scholarship (SKOL-ur-ship)—a grant of money that helps a student pay for college

To Learn More

Bernstein, Ross. *Randy Moss, Star Wide Receiver.* Sports Reports. Berkeley Heights, N.J.: Enslow, 2001.

Stewart, Mark. *Randy Moss: First in Flight.* Football's New Wave. Brookfield, Conn.: Millbrook Press, 2000.

Temple, Bob. *Randy Moss.* Sports Superstars. Chanhassen, Minn.: Child's World, 2001.

Thornley, Stew. *Jerry Rice: Star Wide Receiver.* Sports Reports. Springfield, N.J.: Enslow, 1998.

Useful Addresses

Pro Football Hall of Fame
2121 George Halas Drive NW
Canton, OH 44708

Randy Moss
c/o Minnesota Vikings
9520 Viking Drive
Eden Prairie, MN 55344

Internet Sites

CNN/SI—Randy Moss
http://sportsillustrated.cnn.com/football/nfl/
    players/4262/index.html

Minnesota Vikings
http://www.vikings.com

Mosszone.com
http://mosszone.com

NFL.com
http://nfl.com

Index